LORD Forgive Me

PRAYERS OF CONFESSION
CYCLE C

DAVID L. WADE

C.S.S. Publishing Co., Inc.
Lima, Ohio

LORD, FORGIVE ME, CYCLE C

Reprinted 2002

Copyright © 1988 by
CSS Publishing Company, Inc.
Lima, Ohio

The original purchaser may photocopy material in this publication for use as it was intended (i.e., worship material for worship use; educational material for classroom use; dramatic material for staging or production). No additional permission is required from the publisher for such copying by the original purchaser only. Inquiries should be addressed to: Permissions, CSS Publishing Company, Inc., P.O. Box 4503, Lima, Ohio 45802-4503.

Library of Congress Cataloging-in-Publication Data

Wade, David L., 1940-
   Lord forgive me.
   Includes index.
   1. Prayers. 2. General confession (Prayers) I. Title.
BV250.W27   1988   264'.13   88-4344
ISBN 1-55673-067-5

For more information about CSS Publishing Company resources, visit our website at www.csspub.com or e-mail us at custserv@csspub.com or call (800) 241-4056.

ISBN 1-55673-067-5   PRINTED IN U.S.A.

Table of Contents

About the Author	4
Preface	5
Acknowledgments	6
Suggestions for Use	7

The Advent Season	9
The Christmas Season	13
The Epiphany Season	18
The Lenten Season	28
The Easter Season	38
Calendar index for the Sundays after Pentecost Sunday	48
The Sundays after The Day of Pentecost	50

Special Days

Christmas Eve/Day	13
New Year's Eve/Day	14
Holy Name of Jesus	16
The Baptism of Our Lord	19
The Transfiguration of Our Lord	27
Ash Wednesday	28
Sunday of the Passion	34
Palm Sunday	35
Maundy Thursday	36
Good Friday	37
The Resurrection of Our Lord	38
Ascension Day/Sunday	45
The Day of Pentecost	46
The Holy Trinity	47
Christ the King	76
Reformation Sunday	77
All Saints' Sunday/All Saints' Day	78
Thanksgiving Eve/Day	79
Mother's Day	80
Annual Meeting	81
Installation of Church Officers	82

About The Author

Dave Wade tries to exercise creativity in his ministry to church and community. In addition to prayers of confession like these for each Sunday of the year, he frequently plans and leads folk worship services with guitar or banjo, and has on several occasions presented "sermons in song" with original as well as gathered materials. He occasionally performs for community as well as congregational events.

He serves denominationally and ecumenically as well as in the local congregation. He is currently a member of the Board of Directors of the Rocky Mountain Conference of the United Church of Christ, an officer of the Wyoming Association of that Conference, and represents his Association on the boards of the Wyoming Church Coalition and Wyoming Ministries in Higher Education. He is currently serving his first elected term as a member and officer of the Board of Trustees of Western Wyoming Community College in Rock Springs.

In addition to writing and music, his interests include reading, camping and fishing in the wide-open Western spaces.

Preface

As a campus minister (United Ministries at Ball State University) during the 1970s, I was impressed by the work of a Lutheran colleague, Roger Sasse (Center for University Ministries at Indiana University), especially in the area of worship. He created a new service for each week, after reflecting with other participants on the proposed theme and Scripture lessons for the service, including each week what he referred to as a "Call to Honesty." For several years, and with his permission, I *borrowed* his writings for use in worship with students. Eventually, I began to create my own prayers of Confession, related to the Scripture lessons and worship theme for the day. These efforts met with success among the United Ministries student community, and on my return to parish ministry in 1982, I continued the practice of writing prayers of Confession in contemporary style and language.

This selection follows the Common, Lutheran, and Roman Catholic Lectionaries for Cycle C. I offer them as worship aids to congregations and pastors who would like to try something a bit more contemporary in their worship life, and as aids to personal devotion for individuals.

David L. Wade
Rock Springs, Wyoming
May 1, 1986

Acknowledgments

My thanks to Jean Wade, my spouse and a constant encourager of creativity in life and work;

To Kathy Smith, my faithful manuscript typist and proofreader;

And to the members of First Congregational Church, who say they miss the prayers when they are absent from a Sunday Bulletin.

Suggestions for Use

These Prayers of Confession were written for and used in corporate worship at the First Congregational Church, United Church of Christ in Rock Springs, Wyoming. They are written in the first person, to be read by the congregation in unison, following a pastoral Call to Confession, and followed by both Pastoral and Congregational Assurances of Pardon. The intent of the first-person style is to affirm that, as we gather for worship, we are both individual seekers and believers and also the Body of Christ. Our sins and failings are our own, but they are also universally human. The first-person style makes it more difficult for us to say "They needed that" or "That doesn't apply to me"! It is much easier for us to "cop out" when reading or hearing a traditional, general Prayer of Confession.

As with any creative effort, the prayers vary in many ways, not only from traditional Confessions, but from each other. They may focus on the primary theme of the Scripture passage — the Gospel for the day — or they may pick up on a secondary or even tertiary theme. In a few cases, the focus is on the day itself, rather than the actual words of Scripture.

The personal style, while intended for use by a corporate, worshiping community, does open them up to different kinds of usage. Some possibilities might include: personal preparation for corporate worship through printing in Sunday worship folders, or "in advance" through inclusion in weekly bulletins or newsletters; as a focus for lectionary study groups or in sermon or homily preparation; as an aid to personal devotions; or in other ways that you might devise to suit your own congregation or situation.

Regardless of the way in which you might choose to use them, my hope is that you will find them meaningful in your life and ministry.

Additional Note Concerning the present volume

This second volume of Prayers of Confession also comes out of the life of the First Congregational Church, United Church of Christ in Rock Springs, Wyoming.

Most of these prayers have been used in Sunday worship as unison Confessions of Sin. The first-person style allows most worshipers to take them personally, while the unison reading affirms the common sins of humanity. Their reflection of the Gospel of the Day helps keep them from becoming trivial, and helps keep me from "riding hobby horses."

Others may find them helpful in the study of Scripture, or as preparation for worship — and I hope, as an encouragement to be creative and personal in their own approach to God and each other.

Advent 1

Luke 21:25-36

"Be Prepared."
    So say the Boy Scouts.
"Watch the market."
    So says Wall Street.
"Make a will."
    So say the lawyers.
"Watch for signs."
    So says Jesus.
I try to be ready for anything,
    But I can't put much stock
        In that Apocalyptic stuff
            . . . Signs
                . . . Portents
                    . . . Prophets
                        . . . The End of The World.
So many have tried
    And so many have been wrong!
I read this stuff
    But I don't know what to do with it!
I plan and prepare for life
                . . . and death
        As best I can,
And I trust that God is in charge!
Lord, forgive me for taking your word lightly
    And teach me to prepare my heart,
                My soul,
        For the coming of Jesus
                At Christmas
        And at Judgment.
                Amen

Advent 2

Luke 3:1-6

Peace . . . Everybody wants it!
  It's like motherhood
          Or the flag
          Or apple pie . . .
    Everybody's in favor!
  At home . . .
       "Can I have a little peace?"
       "Let's have some peace and quiet!"
       "It sure is peaceful tonight."
  At work
    At school
      At play.
  It's more rewarding
    More fun
      When things are peaceful,
But is the way to peace found through force?
  Peacekeeping forces . . . The Marines!
  "Peacekeeper" missiles . . . Nuclear weapons
  "The Colt 'Peacemaker' " . . . Hand guns!
Ironic, isn't it?
  That we have to force peace on others?
    Our peace
        (Pax Americana)
    My peace
        (*You* be quiet!)
  The Prince of Peace had no such things.
    No power
      No army
        No guns
  (Maybe that's why we don't have it,
    He didn't force it on us!)
Lord, forgive me my "breaches of the peace,"
    My temper,
      My desires
        My willingness to "fight for peace,"
  And give me *your* peace
      Of heart
        Of mind
          Of body
            . . . And, of soul . . .
  For the sake of the Prince who comes at Christmas.
                Amen

Advent 3

Luke 3:7-18

I love you!
    I also love cookies
        And presents
        And Christmas
        And cuddly animals
        And new cars
        And crisp snow
        And warm sunshine
           . . . And God.
    I use the word love so casually
        To mean affection
           Or liking
           Or enjoyment
           Or satisfaction
           Or
              . . . really . . .
                    nothing,
    That it doesn't mean anything!
Love is Hollywood romance
    And it's casual enjoyment,
  But shouldn't it be more?
The Bible says love is:
        Patient and kind —
        Not arrogant or rude —
        Forgiving and accepting —
        Self-effacing and other-building —
        And constant . . .
           Maybe most of all
           . . . Constant.
Love is God in Christ
        Giving himself for us.
Lord, forgive my casual use of the word
    And my casual abuse of its meaning.
  Forgive my self- and selfish-love,
    And teach me your true love . . .
            The love that never ends.
        In the name of Jesus who loves even me.
                  Amen

Advent 4

Luke 1:39-47

Christmas Time!
        Such a joyous time!
A Christmas tree
        With decorations and lights —
Giving presents
        Receiving presents
Eating a big meal —
        No school
No work
        Snow
            Skiing
            Snowmobiling
            Tubing,
    But are we forgetting what Christmas really is?
Lord, forgive me for taking advantage of Christmas.
        Help me to remember
    That your Son,
        Jesus Christ,
            Was born on this day,
    To teach me all about your love!
    To bring me your love!
    To save me with His love!

Praise God, Father, Son and Holy Spirit
        For all the love you send at Christmas time.
                Amen

The Nativity of Our Lord
(Christmas Eve/Christmas Day)

John 1:1-14

"The Word . . . Dwelt among us."
   The Word . . .
           The Christ,
      Lives on my street!
        Even in my house!
But I don't see him.
         I see creches and trees.
         I see John and Mary.
         I see Grandpa and Sis.
         I see joy in giving and receiving.
   I see . . .
           At least in my mind's eye . . .
              The Babe of Bethlehem,
   But Emmanuel?
               God-With-Us?
                    Here?
                           Now?
            The Word Made Flesh
                Among *us*?
Yet, isn't that what Christmas means?
Christ with us
             Christ in us
                     Even now?
Lord, forgive my blindness to your presence
      Here and now
            In me and those I meet,
    Teach me to look for you
        And to find you
   In my heart and my neighborhood
On Christmas Day and every day.
                     Amen

New Year's Eve/Day

Luke 13:6-9

A New Year —
 A new start —
 A clean slate —
 A fresh page on the calendar —
 Resolutions to change ways —
 Plans to do things differently —
A new year.
 After the break of holidays,
  The joys of Christmas,
   The celebrations of New Year's Eve,
   (The football of New Year's Day)
  Back to work — refreshed — or exhausted!
 A new year.
My new year
 But I bring my old self into it.
  My hopes — and my fears . . .
  My dreams — and my debts . . .
  My triumphs — and my defeats.
A new year.
 Like a new wallet —
  Clean, empty, smooth, unmarked,
   But soon filled with old junk!
  Notes, pictures, cards — obligations and memories,
 Fat, lumpy, messy with life.
A new year.
 Lord, forgive the baggage I carry into it
  And help me to make a new start,
   So that I can greet the new year
  With a new me —
 One in tune with you and your world
Through Jesus Christ, My Lord.
  Amen

Christmas 1 • The Holy Family (RC)
Luke 2:41-52

New wine
    Or old grape juice?
        Fresh
        Bubbly
        Scintillating
        Exciting
        Intoxicating,
    Or
        Dull
        Prosaic
        Flat
        Boring.
Christ brings the taste of new wine,
    Filling our spirits,
    Bubbling out over all whom we meet,
    Making life an adventure,
    Giving us the joy of living,
But I often receive him like grape juice
    Healthy,
        But with no excitement
            No joy
            No life!
Maybe I'm afraid he'll burst my old skin,
        Make me unfit for use,
        Ruin me for my friends
            My work . . .
(Or change me from a caterpillar to a butterfly . . .
    Make me leave my old life behind,
        Fly away freely
            Frighteningly . . .
        Away from everything I know
            Into the great unknown!)
Lord, forgive me for making your wine go flat,
        For being afraid to drink it deeply
            And experience your Eternal Life
                Here
And Now!
    Give me the courage
        To reach for the intoxication of Your Spirit
            And follow You
                For Jesus' sake
                    . . . And my own.
                    Amen

The Holy Name of Jesus

Luke 2:15-21

Names have power,
  Names have meaning,
    Names determine who we are,
        How we see ourselves
        How we see others.
    A strong name,
      A common name,
        A "wimpy" name,
      A family name,
          An unusual name . . .
  All give us something to live up to
      . . . Or to live down!
The name of Jesus
    It means "Yahweh Saves,"
    It communicates Love
          Redemption
          Salvation.
    It stands for all I believe,
    It gives me strength and power.
Lord, forgive me when I take your name lightly
          . . . Or in vain . . .
  And teach me
    Give me
      The power of the name of Jesus.
        — Blessed be that name.
                Amen

Christmas 2

John 1:1-18

My world is in darkness.
    The darkness of doubt —
    The darkness of fear —
    The darkness of ignorance —
    The darkness of hate —
              War
                      Suspicion
                          Mistrust.
  It's hard to see clearly . . .
                        I need light!
  "One little candle" would help,
But a floodlight would be better!
    Something to eliminate shadows,
        To brighten corners,
        To make all things clear,
Unfortunately
        "This little light of mine"
    Is often not enough.
                I need more!
Lord, forgive me for not recognizing,
        Not utilizing
    The Light of the World.
Open my eyes
    Light my way,
And let all things be clear
        For Jesus' sake
            And the sake of the world.
                      Amen

The Epiphany of Our Lord
(January 6)

Matthew 2:1-12

"Where is he?"
    . . . Good question!
                I sometimes wonder myself!
Where is the Christ in the midst of the world?
    Where is he when
             Nations wage war with each other?
             Leaders lie and cheat the public?
             Earthquakes and floods destroy lands?
             People starve in the midst of plenty?
             Husbands beat wives?
                Parents abuse children?
    Where?
        Wise people still seek him
          . . . And some . . .
                  (I pray I may be one)
           Find him!
Lord, forgive my lack of faith,
    My refusal to seek your presence,
    And grant me the perseverance to find you
    And the grace to be found
        By Jesus,
            My Lord.
                Amen

The Baptism of Our Lord
(Epiphany 1 • Ordinary Time 1)

Luke 3:15-16, 21-22

The Holy Spirit . . .
                That's still a puzzle to me!
    I know it
        (him)
            (her)
        As the third part of the Trinity.
I say the words in the creeds and statements,
                But what does it mean?
    I don't think
             (I don't *want* to think)
      It's that showy
             Theatrical
      Stuff,
           Like speaking in tongues
           Rolling on the floor in "ecstasy."
    I don't think
             (I don't *want* to think)
      It's spiritualistic
           Communing with the "dearly departed"
      Stuff
           Or demonic
              "Exorcist"-like
                  Activity.
But then what is it
        (he)
            (she)?
Maybe I should just say the words
        (With my fingers crossed)
                  And forget it!
Lord, forgive my rational demands
        My insistence on dotting "i" 's,
            Crossing "t" 's,
            Controlling through knowledge.
    And give me the simple faith
        To accept what I don't understand
           And live by it,
                For Jesus' sake.
                      Amen

Epiphany 2 • Ordinary Time 2

John 2:1-12

Sometimes I'm not religious enough!
   I neglect the duties and obligations I have
      Like worship attendance,
      Like stewardship,
      Like growing in wisdom and Christian life,
      Like prayer and Bible study and meditation,
      Like teaching my children . . . and my friends,
      Like sharing my faith with others.
   I hide my church affiliation
      . . . and my Lord . . .
     So I won't put people off,
         Make them think I'm strange — a fanatic
         Embarrass myself.
   But sometimes I'm too religious!
      I make judgments about people,
      I separate myself from them,
     Because their faith is different from mine,
 I react piously instead of personally;
     Too Much . . . Or Not Enough!

Lord, forgive me for being concerned about religion,
        About the outward signs
   (Mine . . . or someone else's),
And help me to focus more on your will than my image.
Let me leave the judging to you
     And accept others as your people
      While I try to live up to your expectations,
         For Jesus' sake.
            Amen

Epiphany 3 • Ordinary Time 3

Luke 4:14-21

Jesus sure was self-confident!
．．． I wish I was!
He could teach
　　　　Proclaim
　　　　　Speak and act
　　　　　　　Knowing he was right!
I'm so often afraid that I'm wrong!
　　　．．． Or not knowledgable enough
　　　．．． Or misinformed
　　　．．． Or just not sure!
I'm afraid of the reactions of others,
　　Afraid of saying
　　　　Doing
　　　．．． Something stupid,
　　So I hide in the crowd
　　　　Keep my mouth shut
　　　．．． And complain afterwards!
Lord, forgive me my fears
　　　　Of the reactions of others
　　And give me the power of the Spirit
　　　　So I may speak and act boldly
　　　　　　For Jesus' sake.
　　　　　　　　　Amen

Epiphany 4 • Ordinary Time 4

Luke 4:21-30

So quickly they forget!
   One minute they're impressed —
               Praising Jesus;
   The next minute they turn on him —
               Try to kill him!
      It just goes to show you
                  You can't trust people!
      No wonder I keep my real self hidden —
            Watch what I say.
      No wonder I don't want to risk.
            I play my cards close to my chest.
            I protect myself
                  Until I really know —
                        Really trust people,
                  (And even then, I'm careful!)
Lord, forgive my caution —
      My unwillingness to risk
      And teach me to open myself —
            Give of myself
                        Freely —
                  Trusting in you for my safety,
                              In Jesus' name.
                                    Amen

Epiphany 5 • Ordinary Time 5

Luke 5:1-11

I Belong!
    I belong to the church,
        The church of Jesus Christ
The eternal fellowship of God.
    I have promised myself to Christ and his church,
        To show his love to all people,
            To support his work on earth,
                To learn and grow in his ways.
    But I also belong to the world,
        To my family,
           To my friends,
              To my job,
                  To my country,
And sometimes my "belongings" conflict —
    (Both the things I belong to
            . . . And the things that belong to me!)
    My loyalties are divided,
        My emotions are mixed,
           My priorities are confused.

Lord, forgive me my "doublemindedness,"
    And help me to see what's most important
        (In this world and in your kingdom).
    Help me to juggle my responsibilities,
        To meet my obligations,
           To fulfill my promises,
              To people
              To life
              To the church
                      And to you,
              For Jesus' sake.
                      Amen

Epiphany 6 • Ordinary Time 6

Luke 6:17-26

Lord, I am blessed with so much!
   I own all the things that make life good:
      A home (or at least a place to live),
      Furnishings to make it comfortable,
      A bathroom . . . or two or three,
      Books and records and tapes,
      Radios and TVs and stereos,
      Cars and trucks and boats and snow machines,
      Golf clubs and tennis rackets and skis.
   I have in my possession
      (Or I can get)
      Nearly everything and anything I want.
Why then do I feel poor?
Why do I envy what others have?
      Bigger homes —
      Newer cars —
      Wide-screen TVs —
      More money —
      More leisure —
      Less work???
How can I look at those who have so little,
   And still cry, "Woe is me"?
Do I own my possessions,
          Or do they own me?
Do I determine my life,
          Or is it determined by things?
Is my life a blessing,
          Or is it a curse?

Lord, forgive me for my mixed-up values,
   For my uncertainty,
   For putting things before people,
   . . . And especially before you.
Help me to straighten out my life —
   To free myself from slavery to my possessions.
   Free me for life in your kingdom,
                    For Jesus' sake.
                       Amen

Epiphany 7 • Ordinary Time 7

Luke 6:27-38

Love my enemies?
    Do good to those who hate me?
        You've got to be kidding!
    That's unnatural!
        That's un-American!
            That's . . . impossible!
I have to protect myself!
I have to look after myself!
    I have to hit back —
        Be strong.
    How else will I get any respect?
    How else will I have any peace?
If I always give in
        People will take advantage of me!
    I'll look like . . .
        . . . I'll be . . .
            A wimp!
    A strong stance —
        A strong defense
    Is the only way to live!

Lord, forgive my aggressive nature —
    My rejection of your values
And teach me your ways.
    Give me your strength,
        That I may live a life of love
            And conquer fear and hatred,
                In Jesus' name.
                      Amen

Epiphany 8 • Ordinary Time 8

Luke 6:39-49

How come the speck in your eye
                Is so much easier to see
        Than the log in mine?
Your faults are major . . . and clear.
            Mine are minor . . . and hidden.
You're stubborn!   I'm strong minded.
You're stingy!   I'm fiscally responsible.
You're wild!   I'm fun-loving.
You're fat!   I'm "pleasantly plump."
You're crazy!   I'm eccentric.
And when you try to point out my faults,
        I can tell . . .
              . . . You exaggerate!

Lord, forgive me for my criticism of others,
        And my blindness toward myself.
    Teach me to see more clearly
        To speak more positively,
    And to trust in your grace
            For myself
        And for my brother/sister.
                Amen

The Transfiguration of Our Lord

Luke 9:28-35

Lord, I want things to last!
                An ice cream cone . . .
                A relationship . . .
                A car . . .
                A moment of insight . . .
                A pair of shoes . . .
                Love . . .
                A job . . .
                A special moment,
        But things keep slipping away!
"The nearer your destination,
    The more you're slip-sliding away."*
                Times change.
                People change.
                Children grow.
                Families expand . . . and contract.
                Old things disappear.
                New opportunities beckon.
I'm torn between holding on to the familiar —
    And getting the newest —
        The best
            Of everything.

Lord, forgive me for holding on to the past,
        For milking it beyond its capacity to satisfy.
Help me to savor the moment,
    To release it
    And to be open to today's fresh experience.
Open my eyes
        And my life,
            For Jesus' sake.
                Amen

*"Slip-Sliding Away"
Copyright 1977 Paul Simon

Ash Wednesday

Matthew 6:1-6, 16-21

"Don't practice your piety in public
 In order to impress people."
I need to hear that sometimes.
  Sometimes I go to church,
   Pray in restaurants,
   Show my religion,
  In order to keep up appearances
   Because it's expected of me.
But . . .
  Perhaps more often,
   I'm guilty of keeping my faith a secret.
 I *don't* make a witness.
  I *don't* show myself to be Christian.
   I don't want to be embarrassed
    Or embarrass others,
  So I pretend to be like everyone else
   . . . And deny my Lord.

Lord, forgive me for flaunting my religiousness,
 And for hiding my faith,
 And help me to be your person
  Honestly,
  Naturally,
   In all times and places,
    For Jesus' sake.
     Amen

Lent 1

Luke 4:1-13

Lord, I'm tempted!
        Every day, almost every hour!
    Tempted to cheat
        To lie
        To steal;
    Tempted to overdo
            In eating
                Or drinking;
    Tempted to overvalue things
                And undervalue people;
    Tempted to be less than I could be.
Some temptations are obvious and easy to avoid:
        (Well, at least *relatively* easy!)
    The temptations to hurt,
        To pay back evil with evil,
        To strike out in anger
            With words
                Or with blows!
Some are more subtle . . .
        "*Everybody* drives over 65,"
        "*Everybody* cheats on taxes . . .
            at least a little!"
Some are downright sneaky!
        "It's for their own good."
        "Father/Mother knows best."
I confess that not only do I not stand firm in temptation,
    I frequently don't even recognize it . . .
        Until it's too late . . . if then!

Lord, help me to recognize how vulnerable I am
            To pressure —
                Or flattery —
                Or pride.
Give me the wisdom to know temptation when it comes
    And the courage to resist it,
        As Jesus did.
            I ask it in his name.
                  Amen

Lent 2

Luke 13:31-35

Jesus sure could be hard on people!
  Here he is talking about "Jerusalem"
        The city . . .
    But really, his own people
    Killing prophets —
    Stoning messengers from God —
        Strange behavior for the Holy City!
I'm sure glad we don't do that kind of thing!
I wouldn't reject God's messengers
   . . . Unless, of course,
        They meddled too much!
    Saying America is an oppressor;
    Saying our people aren't free —
        Happy —
        Content;
    Saying we're not always on the right side;
    Saying there are problems
        Sins
          In our society;
    Tearing down what our ancestors —
        Our parents —
          . . . Even we
    Worked so hard to build,
But anybody who'd do something like that . . .
        Attack our values —
        Our way of life —
        Our precious beliefs,
    Couldn't be from God anyway!!!
   . . . Could they?
        (Was *that* what Jesus meant?)
Lord, forgive my moral superiority —
    My assumption that I'm not like them —
      . . . Those Jesus spoke about . . .
   And remind me both of my sin
      And of your forgiveness,
        For Jesus' sake.
          Amen

Lent 3

Luke 13:1-9

I have so many blessings!
    Life —
        Health . . . at least relatively —
        Affluence . . . compared to many —
        Love —
          Comfort —
          Plenty.
I may not always have everything I want,
    But rarely do I not have what I need!
And my blessings are not only material!
    I have your presence —
        Your promise —
            The comfort of your Word —
            The support of your
                church —
                The assurance of your
                love,
    But I take all these things for granted.
I mumble and groan
        Like the Israelites in the desert.
I whine and complain
        Like a little kid who doesn't get his way.
I forget past blessings —
    Future promises —
        In the face of present disappointments.

Lord, forgive my petulance —
        My lack of gratitude —
        My childish preoccupation with self —
And teach me to honor you for your gifts
    . . . And lead me to give in response . . .
                To be more worthy of your gifts,
                      For Jesus' sake.
                          Amen

Lent 4

Luke 15:11-32

I want my own way,
    And sometimes I don't care how I get it!
Oh, I don't lie or cheat for it
    (At least not intentionally),
    But I do put on the pressure!
    I manipulate people
                  . . . Or at least, try to.
I use Guilt . . .
        Anger . . .
           Fear . . .
              Duty . . .
                  . . . Even Love,
    As weapons . . .
        Ways to move people,
    Yet I fiercely resent anyone using *me* . . .
        Trying to manipulate *me* to *their* ends.

Lord, forgive me for using people
        . . . Instead of loving them.
    Help me to see them as brothers and sisters
        . . . As people, not objects.
    Let me ask "How can I love you?"
        . . . Rather than "How can I use you?"
    Let my "rule" be Golden
        . . . As Jesus' was,
    And use me in his work,
                For his sake.
                    Amen

Lent 5

John 12:1-8

If I could have been there!
    At Lazarus' house
        To see Mary anoint his feet,
            I'd have been awestruck;
            I'd have rebuked Judas.
                      I think I would,
                          anyway!
If I could have been there!
    When He entered Jerusalem
        I'd have waved my palm;
        I'd have shouted "Hosanna."
                      I think I would,
                          anyway!
If I could have been there!
    At the Last Supper
        I'd have shared the bread and wine;
        I'd have known the betrayer.
                      I think I would,
                          anyway!
If I could have been there!
    At His arrest
    His trial
    His crucifixion,
        I'd have spoken for him;
        I'd have stayed with him.
                      I think I would,
                          anyway!
If I could have been there!

Lord, forgive me for judging others
    Long after the fact,
        When I don't share their experience,
And for assuming that I am better,
        Stronger,
        More faithful
                . . . Than they are.
    Teach me to accept my own fears
            And your love,
        Despite my failings,
            In Jesus' name.
                Amen

Sunday of the Passion

Luke 22:1; 23:56

What a story!
    From celebration
           . . . To betrayal
           . . . To arrest
           . . . To trial
           . . . To execution,
    All in a night and a day.
Powerful drama,
        But so familiar,
               That I tend to ignore it!
I'm more interested in my *own* story . . .
        My triumphs
        My trials
        My betrayals.
I remember what happened so long ago,
      But deep down inside,
            I say
                "So what?"

Lord, forgive me when I forget
            Your sacrifice
            And your love,
And remind me . . .
          Again and again . . .
            Of the Passion of my Lord,
               For my sake.
                  Amen

Palm Sunday
(When not observed as Sunday of the Passion)

Luke 19:28-40
Matthew 26:14-27, 66

If I had only been there!
   If I could have greeted Jesus
       Coming into Jerusalem!
   If I could have waved my palm branch,
       Laid my coat down for a carpet
       Shouted "Hosanna!"
            (Or Hurray!)
  I would have understood!
    I would have known Jesus
        As Messiah . . .
        As King . . .
        As Savior!
    I would have followed him . . .
       Protected him,
       Tried to save him from his enemies!
I wouldn't have run away in fear!
I wouldn't have hidden!
I wouldn't have denied him!
        . . . Or would I?
I know so much more now than they did then.
   I've read the Gospels;
   I've grown up in the church;
   I've met Jesus as Savior
        As Lord,
     Not as a stranger with a strange message!
  I judge those people
        As "fair weather friends,"
        As cowards,
   But I don't show the bravery in my own life
    That I dream about in Holy Week.
  I don't speak up for my Lord.
  I don't show Christ in my life.

Lord, forgive my judgment of others,
   And my cowardice in the kingdom.
    Give me the courage I seek,
        And the ability to forgive . . . and to love . . .
        That Jesus showed.
   I ask it for the sake of him who died for me.
             Amen

Maundy Thursday

**Luke 22:7-20
John 13:1-15**

The last night Jesus spent with his disciples:
    A common meal . . .
        A commandment . . .
            "DO THIS."
    I can hear Luke's "Do this."
    I get sentimental about the sacrament.
    I wallow in the darkness of the soul.
    I eat and drink with heavy heart,
        Knowing what is to come . . .
And, maybe . . .
        Rejoicing because I know the rest of the story.
    I have trouble with John's story!
        Footwashing!
            A commandment not just to *remember*,
                But to *act*,
                    To *serve*.
    That's a lot harder to hear
            And to do!
    Yet the bread and the wine . . .
        The body and the blood . . .
        Are not ends in themselves,
        But power for service to others!

Lord, forgive me for leaving you in the Upper Room
    For remembering the Last Supper,
    Instead of taking you into my world.
    Grant me the power of your sacrament,
        For a life of service,
                In Jesus' name.
                    Amen

Good Friday

John 18:1 — 19:42

The cavalry didn't show up over the hill!
   No eleventh hour call from the warden!
      No reprieve.
TRIAL
            SENTENCE
                        EXECUTION
            It's over.
               Jesus is dead.
   My God, why?
            Wasn't there some other way?
                  Couldn't you have saved him?
            (Is that what *I* have to expect?
                  False accusations?
                  Persecution?
                     Death?)
         "If it be thy will,
            Let this cup pass from me!"

Lord, forgive me for taking this day too lightly,
         For not appreciating the sacrifice
                  Which was Jesus'
                     Which could be mine.
   Help me to say
            . . . and mean . . .
      "Nonetheless, Thy will be done"
   for "Into your hands, I commit my spirit."
                           Amen

The Resurrection of Our Lord

John 20:1-18

Colored eggs —
        Frilly baskets and fancy bonnets —
    Plush bunnies and dyed chicks —
           Lamb — or ham — and lots of candy;
        We know it's Easter . . .
                      It's been advertised!
    But what do these things have to do with
        R E S U R R E C T I O N?
    (Some of them, a little, symbolically,
                Some of them . . . not much!)
Like Christmas, Easter's been
    Commercialized —
        Mechanized —
           Sanitized —
                To where it's "cute,"
    Instead of a matter of life and death . . .
Eternal life
                . . . Or eternal death!

Lord, I lose sight of your truths —
            Your insights —
            Your revelation,
    Because I trivialize the important things
    And lionize the trivial ones!
Forgive me my lack of understanding —
        My doubts —
               My unbelief in the face of your
                    miracles,
    And help me to grasp the fact of the Resurrection,
        For Jesus,
                And for me.
                      Amen

Easter 2

John 20:19-31

"Peace be with you."
    What a wonderful message!
      And what a difficult one to hear!
   The disciples needed it!
     Their lives were anything but peaceful.
        They were confused,
          Grieving,
          Afraid.
I need it!
    I'm all those things too!
      Confused by the pace of life,
        By changes in values,
        By new technology;
      Grieving the loss of old ways —
          Of good friends;
      Afraid of the future,
        Of demands made on me,
        Of not living up to expectations.
I need to hear "Peace be with you,"
    But instead I hear
         "There is no peace,"
    And in sight of the peace of God,
      I perish.

Lord, forgive me for not accepting your peace,
    For living in anger and fear,
  And teach me to accept peace,
      To live peace,
      To share peace,
         In the name of the Prince of Peace.
            Amen

Easter 3

John 21:1-14

Easter's over.
　　　　The eggs all eaten
　　　　　　　　(Or made into egg salad).
　　　　The leftovers consumed.
　　　　The finery hung in the closet.
That's it for another year!
　　　　　　　　Might as well go fishing!
So quickly we forget —
　　　　　　　　Forget the celebration of new life;
　　　　　　　　Forget the joy of Easter;
　　　　　　　　Forget the crowded sanctuary;
　　　　　　　　　　Even forget the empty tomb . . .
　　　　　　　　　　　　　　And what it means to us.
　　Our celebrations are quickly over.
　　　　　　Almost before the dust has settled,
　　　　　　　　Or the wrapping paper destroyed,
　　(Or the lilies lost their blooms),
We've moved on to something else . . .
　　　　　　　　An event
　　　　　　　　A worry . . .
　　　　　　　　　　　　　　The next holiday.
　　We don't savor the good things,
　　　　Squeeze the last drop of goodness from them,
　　Instead we experience . . . and we forget.

Lord, forgive us for passing so quickly over the most important
　　　　　　　　Event
　　　　　　　　　　　　Of them all!
　　　　Build us a spirit of Easter . . .
　　　　　　　　Of new life in the Spirit . . .
　　　　　　　　Of eternal life in your kingdom . . .
　　And keep the Resurrection before us,
　　　　　　　　　　For the sake of Him who rose.
　　　　　　　　　　　　　　　　Amen

Easter 4

John 10:22-30

"All we like sheep have gone astray!"
    Familiar words —
        Beautiful words —
            Seasonal words —
                      Offensive words!
    Who's a sheep?
        Not me!
        I'm no dumb sheep!
            Dumb, helpless creatures,
                Always in trouble
                      Easily led (even to destruction),
        Useful, maybe
            For wool
                Or leather
                    Or food,
                          But not desirable!
    I'm no sheep!
        Not me!
I'm smart!
    I'm self-sufficient!
    I'm courageous!
                But I can also be led
                      . . . Or mis-led;
                Fooled;
        Tricked into following the wrong leader,
                The wrong shepherd.

Lord, forgive me my arrogance,
        My quickness to declare what I'm not,
        My failure to recognize what I am.
    Give me the trust,
        The devotion
            Of a sheep,
        Along with the courage
            And compassion
        Of a shepherd
           In the name of the Good Shepherd.
                      Amen

Easter 5

John 13:31-35

"They'll know we are Christians by our love"?
It's a good song.
It's a nice thought,
But how true is it?
We've heard the commandment to love one another . . .
Time and again we've heard it,
But living it is much harder!
I find it hard to love the people I'm closest to . . .
Family: parents, children, brothers and sisters . . .
(At least some of the time).
How can I love people with whom my only connection
Is membership in the church?
Or even less than that . . .
People who share my living space . . .
Town, country, school, work . . .
Or people who only share humanity with me?
I can't love just because I'm supposed to!
I want to love those who will love me back!
I want to love those who are lovable!
I want to love those who won't hurt me —
Disappoint
me —
Reject me!

Help me, Lord!
Forgive me for only loving selfishly,
And teach me to love as you love me . . .
Unconditionally —
Selflessly —
Sacrificially —
Totally,
So the words I sing will be true,
For Jesus' sake,
And for the God who is love.
Amen

Easter 6

John 14:23-29

"When all else fails,
  Read the directions!"
That's a good reminder for me
  . . . That someone else may know better!
  I usually don't believe it . . .
    I'd rather do it my way!
      Even if it's wrong!
  I hate to have anyone
    . . . Even an inanimate sheet of paper . . .
      Tell me what to do.
  I resist taking orders.
  I rebel against authority.
Jesus says,
  "If you love me, you will keep my word."
    (Do my will/Keep my commandments)
  Love is obedience?
    If I find it hard to obey,
      Does that mean I don't love?
    I hope not!

Lord, forgive my arrogance —
  My independence —
  My lack of obedience,
And teach me to hear your word,
    And to keep it,
      For the love of Jesus.
        Amen

Easter 7

John 17:20-26

"That they may all be one,"
    A prayer of Jesus;
        A vision of the Church;
    One that I affirm with my mouth,
        But deny in my heart!
There are just too many differences among churches.
    Some are too formal.
                Some are too free.
    Some are too emotional.
                Some are too cold.
    Some are too pushy.
                Some are too laid back.
    Some are too loud.
                Some are too quiet.
    Some are too liberal.
                Some are too conservative.
People worship
        And witness
    In so many different ways!
I like *my* way!
        Too often I *don't* like,
            Don't understand
                The ways of others!
    And so I see them as strangers,
        Not part of my
             Christian
            Family.

Lord, forgive me for denying the unity of the faith.
    Teach me that unity
        Doesn't demand uniformity,
    And that my way
        And their way,
    May both be your way,
        In Jesus' name, in whom all are one.
            Amen

Ascension Day / Ascension Sunday
(May replace Easter 7)

Luke 24:44, 46-53

I suppose the Ascension of Christ
    Is an important doctrine.
The creeds affirm it.
    Logic demands it.
        (If Jesus' resurrection body was solid
            . . . as Luke says . . .
        It had to go *somewhere*!)
But maybe what is more important
        Than where Jesus went,
    Is what he left behind!
            Understanding of his role —
            Witnesses to the Resurrection —
            The promise of God —
            Power to do God's work —
    That's what I want
        . . . and that's what God has given me!

Lord, forgive me when I doubt and question
    And teach me to look for
        Insight
        More than facts
    That I may tell the story of Jesus,
        As a faithful witness
            To the Resurrection.
                Amen

The Day of Pentecost

John 14:8-17, 25-27 (C)
John 15:26-27, 16:4b-11 (L)
John 20:19-23 (RC)
Acts 2:1-3

Pentecost
    A strange word —
             A strange story!
    Visions of flames —
        Speaking in other languages —
        3,000 converts!
Sounds like the observers had a point!
              (Maybe they *were* all drunk . . .
              Or high on something!)
I don't know what to think about this "Spirit"!
    Sounds kind of spooky!
    If it/he/whatever makes people do crazy things,
        I'm not sure I want it!
Shouldn't worship,
        Religion
            Be dignified?
    On the other hand,
        I could stand a little enthusiasm —
            A little excitement —
            In my faith.
        Nothing crazy . . .
              No rolling in the aisles —
              No shouting "Amen" —
              No speaking in tongues,
        Just some evidence that faith is not
            DEAD
            or
            DEADLY!

Lord, forgive me my fear of the unknown,
            Of receiving your Spirit
                And His Power,
    And come upon me,
             Inspiring me —
            Empowering me —
            Enabling me to do wondrous things,
                In your name,
                And to your glory.
                    Amen

The Holy Trinity

John 16:12-15

Three in One —
    That's an oil, isn't it?
Does it matter, really, what I believe?
    I mean the specifics —
        The doctrines . . .
                The Trinity
                The Virgin Birth
                The Immaculate
                    Conception
    . . . How many angels can dance on a pin head?
What does that have to do
        With living a Christian life?
        With being a Christian?
    WHO CARES?
        . . . Except maybe theologians in
            ivory towers?
Trinitarian
Unitarian
Dualist
    What's the difference?

Lord, forgive my ignorance
    And my apathy
        About you and your nature.
Help me to ask,
    To question,
    To study and learn,
    And most of all
        To work for your kingdom.
        For Jesus' sake,
            (And yours
                And the Spirit's).
                    Amen

Usage Guide for the Sundays After Pentecost

The three lectionaries which the prayers in this book serve locate them differently in the second half of the church year, the Sundays after the Day of Pentecost. The Lutheran lectionary assigns the prayers according to the Sundays after Pentecost. The Pentecost designations which appear in the pages which follow refer to the Lutheran lectionary.

Denominations using the Common lectionary also refer to Sundays in the second half of the church year as Sundays "after Pentecost," but the Scripture texts (and hence the prayers) in this half of the church year are assigned not to Sundays after Pentecost per se, but rather to fixed dates. The Roman Catholic lectionary, which uses the terminology "Sundays in Ordinary Time" during this second half of the church year, also follows this fixed-date system for the assignment of texts. The following chart will indicate the scheme according to which the texts and prayers are assigned:

Common Lectionary	Roman Catholic Lectionary	Fixed-date Assignment
Proper 4	Ordinary Time 9	May 29 — June 4
Proper 5	Ordinary Time 10	June 5-11
Proper 6	Ordinary Time 11	June 12-18
Proper 7	Ordinary Time 12	June 19-25
Proper 8	Ordinary Time 13	June 26 — July 2
Proper 9	Ordinary Time 14	July 3-9
Proper 10	Ordinary Time 15	July 10-16
Proper 11	Ordinary Time 16	July 17-23
Proper 12	Ordinary Time 17	July 24-30
Proper 13	Ordinary Time 18	July 31 — August 6
Proper 14	Ordinary Time 19	August 7-13
Proper 15	Ordinary Time 20	August 14-20
Proper 16	Ordinary Time 21	August 21-27
Proper 17	Ordinary Time 22	August 28 — September 3
Proper 18	Ordinary Time 23	September 4-10
Proper 19	Ordinary Time 24	September 11-17
Proper 20	Ordinary Time 25	September 18-24

Common Lectionary	Roman Catholic Lectionary	Fixed-Date Assignment
Proper 21	Ordinary Time 26	September 25 — October 1
Proper 22	Ordinary Time 27	October 2-8
Proper 23	Ordinary Time 28	October 9-15
Proper 24	Ordinary Time 29	October 16-22
Proper 25	Ordinary Time 30	October 25-29
Proper 26*	Ordinary Time 31**	October 30 — November 5
Proper 27	Ordinary Time 32	November 6-12
Proper 28	Ordinary Time 33	November 13-19
Christ the King	Christ the King	November 20-26

* The Sunday nearest November 1 may be observed as All Saints' Sunday
** When November 1 is a Sunday it is observed as All Saints' Day

Proper 4 • Pentecost 2 • Ordinary Time 9

Luke 7:1-10

I'm only human!
    I make mistakes —
        Faulty judgments —
        Bad decisions.
    I forget things
        (Accidentally or intentionally).
    I mis-assign priorities.
    I promise
        And don't carry through.
    I threaten
        And don't really mean it.
But I also love
    And forgive
        And share.
I'm "only human!"
    But "human" is all there is to be!
    And I'm proud to be it!
Human is humane.
    Human is caring.
        Human is acting for the other.
            Human is a child of God!

Lord, forgive me the shortcomings of humanity,
    My fallibility,
    My weakness,
And lead me to become *more* human
        A better person,
        More like the perfect human,
        My Lord, Jesus Christ,
            In whose name I ask it.
            Amen

Proper 5 • Pentecost 3 • Ordinary Time 10

Luke 7:11-17

"It's a matter of life and death!"
    (It usually isn't, really,
        But I tend to blow things out of proportion!)
   Things may be important to me,
      But they're usually not *that* important!
My priorities are often out of whack . . .
              I put my comfort —
                  My prosperity —
                  My peace of mind —
                  My safety
           Ahead of your issues
                           Like peace —
                           Like justice —
                           Like mercy —
                           Like . . . eternal life!
I'm more concerned with the short term
        Than with the long;
            With my wishes,
        Than with someone else's needs;
            With my comfort,
        Than with someone else's life!

Lord, forgive me for being preoccupied
                        With "Me"
                              And "My,"
And help me to see the real "life and death" matters . . .
        Faith —
            Trust —
                 Hope —
                     Love —
And give me the life
        That transcends death,
     For the sake of Him who did it for me,
        Even Jesus, My Lord.
                      Amen

Proper 6 • Pentecost 4 • Ordinary Time 11

Luke 7:36-50

Other people's faults are so easy to see!
    I can spot them in a minute.
        I can point them out unerringly,
        And I can tell them what they should have done!
                It's so obvious!
They mess up because
        They don't think,
        They don't care,
        They don't know right from wrong,
        They are selfish,
        They're just bad people!
I make mistakes
        Or wrong decisions
                Or overlook things,
    But those are honest mistakes,
        Miscalculations,
        Oversights,
        Examples of wrong rules and
            bad laws!

Lord, forgive my self-righteousness,
    My eagerness to judge others and forgive myself
        (Frequently for the same actions);
    And help me to be easier on others —
        To lead them to righteousness
            Instead of damning them to Hell;
    And to be harder on myself,
        To recognize my sins for what they are . . .
            Examples of my own imperfection
            My rebellion;
    And lead me to repent;
    And to accept the forgiveness you have promised me,
            In Jesus' name.
                Amen

Proper 7 • Pentecost 5 • Ordinary Time 12

Luke 9:18-24

The church is one . . .
                    But she has so many parts!
    Methodist
      Baptist
        Catholic
          Fundamental
            Conservative
              Liberal
                Orthodox
                  Reformed
                Free
              Social
            Political
          Spiritual
        American
      Russian
    Greek
                    Is it any wonder that I can't see the one-ness?
I'm separated from my sisters and brothers in so many ways . . .
            Where I live . . .
            What language I speak . . .
                (Whether I say "debts" or "trespasses")
            What hymns I sing . . .
            What creeds I recite . . .
That I see my church
              Rather than your church,
And when I do that
    I see "us" and "them"
            Instead of just US.

Lord, forgive my exclusiveness . . .
        My selfishness . . .
        My assurance that my way is the best way,
And help me to see myself as your servant . . .
                One of many . . .
                          All equal . . .
                          All worthy . . .
                (At least as worthy as I am),
        And as a part of your church,
            That encompasses all
                And mirrors the unity of her Lord,
                      Jesus, the Christ. Amen

Proper 8 • Pentecost 6 • Ordinary Time 13

Luke 9:51-62

Jesus says, "Follow Me!"
    I say, "OK,
    But I have a few things to do first!"
My calendar is always full.
    I have so many responsibilities:
        Home —
        Family —
        Work —
        Play —
    And they are all important!
I've made promises
    And, of course, I must keep them!
  But do I prioritize?
    Do I honor them in order of importance?
    Do I choose wisely?
  Or do I try to do everything,
    And miss what's *really* important,
      Because I have no more time?
Jesus says, "The kingdom comes first!"
  I agree
    . . . But it's usually *my* kingdom,
              Not his!

Lord, forgive me for my busyness
      Which so often interferes with your
      business,
  And teach me to hear your call,
    And to follow . . .
        Now.
        Amen

Proper 9 • Pentecost 7 • Ordinary Time 14

Luke 10:1-12, 17-20

Our Father Who art in Heaven . . .
    Lord God of Hosts . . .
        King of Kings . . .
            Most of my "God words"
              Are "man words" . . .
        Male imagery
           Full of power and authority
                (Real macho stuff!)
And because of my God language,
    I tend to be chauvinistic
        (Whether I'm male or female).
    I forget the other side of God
        (Or, at least, I seem to):
The nurturing,
    Comforting,
    Forgiving,
    Enfolding
        Nature of God . . .
            The virtues that I think of as feminine
    (Though they're not, really . . .
        Or at least, not only . . .)

Lord, (there I go again)
    Forgive me for my unthinking use of language,
        For the ways in which I limit you
            By restricting my image of you,
    And for the unthinking ways in which I exclude people . . .
        My brothers and sisters
            (Especially my sisters)
        From your household.
    Help me to know that my words can't contain you
        And to learn to live so that my thoughts and actions
            Embrace *all* your people
                For the Redeemer's sake,
            The One who wiped out all our differences.
                      Amen

Proper 10 • Pentecost 8 • Ordinary Time 15

Luke 10:25-37

The Good Samaritan . . .
    It's a nice story:
  This guy stops and helps an injured traveler,
    Gives him first aid,
    Takes him to a hotel
    (Hospitals hadn't been invented yet),
    Offers to pay his bill . . .
                    UNREAL!
What about the risks?
    The Samaritan could have been
      mugged.
    He certainly lost a lot of time!
    He could have been sued,
  Or accused of beating the guy himself!
    He had to get messy.
    He was out money that he might not
      get back.
Was it worth taking the chance?
I probably wouldn't do it!
    I'd be afraid
      Of the mess —
      Of losing money —
      Losing time —
      Of not knowing what to do!
"I'd rather not get involved"
    In the pain —
    The dirt —
    The poverty —
    The needs of the world.

Lord, forgive my caution,
  My fear
  My rationalizations
      For not loving.
  Teach me to see clearly,
    To act swiftly,
    To be the Samaritan,
    To show others the love you show me,
      Not because of who I am,
      But because of who you are,
        And for Jesus' sake.
              Amen

Proper 11 • Pentecost 9 • Ordinary Time 16

Luke 10:38-42

Run, run, run!
    Work, work, work!
        Busy, busy, busy!
    Every minute of every day,
        There's *something* to do!
            Cleaning,
            Fixing,
            Preparing,
            Organizing,
            Re-arranging,
            Supervising,
                . . . Worrying . . .
    I never seem to get ahead
        Or even keep up!
There's so much to do,
    And so little time to do it,
        That if I stop and do nothing,
            Rest,
            Relax,
            Think,
                . . . Even pray . . .
    I feel guilty.
        I should be doing something!
But You gave us the earth to enjoy,
    As well as to subdue.

Lord, forgive me for the arrogance
    That makes me think *I'm* the only competent one,
    That if I don't do it, it won't get done,
And help me to stop and contemplate
    The wonders of your creation.
Open my spirit to your Spirit
    That I may not only do your will,
        But be your Person,
            For Jesus' sake.
                Amen

Proper 12 • Pentecost 10 • Ordinary Time 17

Luke 11:1-13

The Bible says:
    "Pray without ceasing,"
    "Persist in prayer,"
      . . . All kinds of stuff like that,
  But I don't!
    I guess I rely more on
      "God knows what we need before we ask it,"
      "God knows the sparrow's fall,"
        . . . Those kinds of verses.
I get embarrassed about praying
    (Especially in public),
    Especially if I'm asked to lead a prayer
    (That's the preacher's job!).
  I don't know what to say
      Or how to say it!
I even get nervous when the prayer is too long in worship,
  Or when there is too much silence in it.
Maybe I don't know how to pray
        Or maybe I'm afraid to,
    Afraid of what people will think,
    Afraid my prayer won't be answered
      . . . Or that it *will* be . . .
    And then I'll be stuck!

Lord, forgive me for my fears,
      My halting gestures,
      My lack of perseverance,
  And teach me to pray
        Regularly,
        Freely,
        Faithfully,
        Persistently,
        Honestly,
            In the name of Jesus,
            And for his sake.
                  Amen

Proper 13 • Pentecost 11 • Ordinary Time 18

Luke 12:13-21

"Lay up treasures for yourself."
    The words may be old-fashioned,
        But the idea seems sound to me!
If I don't save,
    Invest,
    Prepare for the future,
        Who will take care of me?
    Social security,
    IRAs,
    Insurance policies,
All the ways I try to anticipate and prepare;
It's all just good common sense!
I worry about the safety of my investments
    . . . Whether Social security will still be there
        when I need it,
    . . . Whether the banks will remain solvent,
    . . . Whether inflation will eat up my retirement
        income,
    . . . Whether the stock market will hold up
    . . . whether my investments are good ones,
But I'm not about to squander my money
Or *not* invest and prepare for the future!
        That would be stupid.
Yet, Jesus said the fool
    Was the one who planned ahead
        Fiscally
    . . . And not spiritually.
    Am I doing that?
        I wonder.

Lord, forgive my distorted priorities,
    As I lay up treasure on earth
        Instead of in heaven,
And teach me to invest myself
    . . . not just my money . . .
    In your kingdom,
        Where the return is sure.
            Amen

Proper 14 • Pentecost 12 • Ordinary Time 19

Luke 12:35-40

"Come, Lord Jesus, be our guest"
                                  I'm not sure I want that!
I'm having enough trouble dealing with the first time!
    I've got a good thing going here!
        I do what I want.
                    (Within reason)
    I make my own decisions.
                    (More or less)
    I make my profit.
                    (Not too much, but enough)
    I've got religion,
                    (Not so much as to be a weirdo,
                            but enough)
        I get along OK!
I'm not sure that I want Jesus,
    Or anyone else, for that matter,
        Messing things up for me!
If he really came back
        There'd be some changes made!
    He'd probably make demands
        About what I have,
        About what I do with it,
        About how I do my job,
            (Or even what my job is),
        About how I live,
            . . . not to mention that judgment stuff!!
I'm doing OK as it is
        (Not great, maybe, but OK).
    I don't need *more* of Jesus!

Lord, forgive me for saying what I don't believe,
        For my hypocrisy in claiming to be your servant
           While putting myself first,
And lead me to want your kingdom to come
        As much as I say I do
            For Jesus' sake,
            And that of the kingdom,
                And my own.
                        Amen

Proper 15 • Pentecost 13 • Ordinary Time 20

Luke 12:49-56

"Woe to those who cry, 'Peace, peace,'
    When there is no Peace."
                    (Jeremiah said that.)
"Peace on earth among people of good will."
                    (The angels said that.)
"I came not to bring peace, but a sword."
                    (Jesus said that.)
    What is this peace?
        Why all the confusion?
        Should I want it?
        How do I get it?
    I try to be a peaceful person,
        A peacemaker,
But my world is so full of conflict!
            Disappointments,
            Arguments,
            Fights,
                Even wars
    That I wonder if it's even possible.
Is the human race naturally warlike?
        Naturally territorial?
        Naturally aggressive?
        Naturally killers?
    When I try to be peaceful,
        Non-aggressive,
I find myself being pushed around!
        Cheated!
        Taken advantage of!
        Walked over!
    Until I lose my temper
        And *demand* respect!
    Is it possible for me to be peaceful?

Lord, forgive me my temper,
    My anger,
    My needless aggression,
And give me peace in my heart
    And in my life,
    So I can help bring peace to my world,
            For its own sake,
            And Jesus'.
                Amen

Proper 16 • Pentecost 14 • Ordinary Time 21

Luke 13:22-30

Discipline!
    That's a dirty word!
    It conjures up pictures of punishment —
        Like standing in the corner,
        Like being sent to my room,
        Like spankings,
        Like doing things I don't want to do,
            Just because someone said I should!
Self-discipline is almost as bad
    . . . Controlling my impulses,
        My desires,
    Denying myself things I want,
        Because they are not good for me,
        Or because I want something else more.
            Work,
            Practice,
            Exercise,
            It all sounds so hard
            . . . So "not fun,"
But I need discipline
        To force me to do what must be done,
        To accomplish worthwhile goals,
        To be what I want to be.
I just don't want it!
I'd rather take it easy.
        Be lazy.
        Float through life!

Lord, forgive me my undisciplined life
    And teach me to set goals
            And work for them
        In my daily life,
        So I can achieve my potential
        And as a Christian,
        So I can be worthy of your calling
           For your kingdom's sake.
                Amen

Proper 17 • Pentecost 15 • Ordinary Time 22

Luke 14:1, 7-14

"Whoever exalts themselves shall be humbled."
   There's some truth in that!
      Somebody is always lying in wait,
         Ready to bring down the mighty,
            Expose the clay feet,
            Puncture the pompous
     Politicians,
       Evangelists,
        Civic leaders,
               All have felt it.
  But the reverse?
"Whoever humbles themselves will be exalted?"
     Not very often!
      Not very likely!
"If you don't blow your own horn
   No one will blow it for you!"
We're taught to know our worth
               And assert it,
   Or we'll be passed over,
            Left behind.

Lord, forgive me for seeking honor and fame
              Instead of seeking to serve,
  And teach me to look for your favor
          In faithful service.
                    For Jesus' sake.
                        Amen

Proper 18 • Pentecost 16 • Ordinary Time 23

Luke 14:25-33

"What will it cost me?"
    That's the first question,
                      The important question,
                      The bottom line.
I want to know the price.
I want to shop around.
I feel sick if I paid too much!
    I'm concerned with economics,
        With responsible use of my money.
I want to know what's involved when I take a job
                      (Volunteer or paid).
        What are the duties?
        What are the hours?
        What are the benefits?
        How much time will it take?
        What are the responsibilities?
    That's good!
        That's being responsible!
            That's effective stewardship!
Then why don't I use it in church?
Why do I say "yes" without thinking it out,
    And get stuck with a bigger job than I intended?
Why do I say "no" without thinking it out,
    And never use my skills or expand my potential?
        Even though I know "You get what you pay for."
Why do I limit my involvement in the kingdom
    . . . Back into it instead of pressing forward . . .
And then find
    Sadly
    "The church isn't very important in my life"?

Lord, forgive me for leaving my brains at the door,
        For not counting the cost of discipleship,
    And for my own cowardice . . .
        For choosing not to pay the whole cost.
Help me to be realistic about your call
            And my response,
            And to become a disciple
                For Jesus' sake.
                    Amen

Proper 19 • Pentecost 17 • Ordinary Time 24
Luke 15:1-10

Lost!
    A poignant word —
    A frightening word —
    A painful word,
Whatever is lost . . .
            An airliner full of people —
            A child —
            A friend or loved one —
            A pet —
            A favorite possession —
            A job —
                . . . Money —
    Whenever something is lost
            There is pain involved,
        Not just for the loser,
        But for all who love him.
Found!
    A joyful word —
    A word of celebration —
    A word that fills life,
Whatever is found . . .
            A pin —
            A toy —
            A bargain —
            Happiness —
                . . . Money —
    Is a cause to celebrate
            Not only for the finder,
            But for all who love her.
I'm sometimes lost
        Physically . . . in strange places,
        Emotionally . . in strong feelings,
        Spiritually . . . in conflicting values and beliefs.

Lord, forgive me for losing my way,
        Losing sight of your path,
        Forgetting that I have been found by you,
    And that I never need to lose myself again.
    Let me rejoice that I am found
        And that others have also been found,
        Through the works of Jesus
            In whose name I pray.
                Amen

Proper 20 • Pentecost 18 • Ordinary Time 25

Luke 16:1-13

Christian ethics!
    My ethics!
        A thorny question!
  Oh, not on the surface!
      Everybody knows what's right!
        But everybody doesn't always agree
            Even on major issues,
                Much less the nitty-gritty of daily decisions!
How do I know what's right for me?
        What is normal?
        What is ethical?
      Business practices considered ethical by some
          May conflict with my religious values.
    Personal habits and behavior I think OK,
        May draw criticism from religious friends . . .
            Either because I'm "too loose"
            Or because I'm too strict!
  So, I do the best I can
      (I think . . .
            I hope . . .)
      Knowing that I often fall short of perfect
            . . . Or even good . . .
      And trust in God's mercy.

Lord, forgive me for my shady practices
        My little deceits
        My failure to treat others
            Always
                As I would have them treat me,
And help me to be an ethical Christian,
            A worthy candidate for your kingdom
                For Jesus' sake.
                    Amen

Proper 21 • Pentecost 19 • Ordinary Time 26

Luke 16:19-31

I want miracles!
I want to be sure!
I want God to break in,
    To do me favors,
    To rescue me from my mistakes,
        My bad decisions,
        The dangers of living,
        The consequences of my sins.
I want miracles for assurance!
    To prove I'm not wasting my time
        In worship,
        In morality,
        In living a decent life,
        In thinking of others!
I want to know I'm on the right track.
I want God to pat me on the head,
    To say, "You've been a good girl/boy,
        Keep it up and everything will be OK!"
But I know she doesn't work that way!
I know I have my instructions.
I know I have the evidence of Jesus,
    And those who have walked in his path.
I just get discouraged,
        Impatient,
        Nervous!

Lord, forgive me my impatience,
    My craving for magic,
    My doubts,
And give me the courage to live in faith,
        To continue to question,
        To be content with ambiguity
            And with your love
    Rather than having an iron-clad guarantee.
Let me follow Jesus
        For his love alone.
            Amen

Proper 22 • Pentecost 20 • Ordinary Time 27
Luke 17:1-10

Have faith!
    I do . . . in some things!
        I have faith . . .
            That my car will start,
            That the sun will come up,
            That I'll be here tomorrow,
            That gravity works,
            That science is accurate.
        I have faith in the laws of nature.
Be faithful!
    I am . . . or I try to be!
        I'm faithful . . .
            To my spouse,
            To my work,
            To my children/parents,
            To my self,
            To my beliefs.
    So much of what I do —
        What I know —Is "on faith."
I continue to live.
I write checks.
I trust people.
        I have faith
            (But I also have niggling doubts),
Especially when it comes to Christian faith.
    I don't know if I want to "live by faith" that way!
        I might have to give up control,
            Take risks,
            "Bet the farm"
        On something I have doubts about!
Is it true?
Is it real?
Is it sure?
        Can I trust God?
            Really?

O Lord, forgive me my doubts,
        My fears,
        My faithlessness
    And increase my faith
            In you,
            In Christ Jesus
    And in the changes he can make in me.
        I ask it in his name.   Amen

Proper 23 • Pentecost 21 • Ordinary Time 28

Luke 17:11-19

"That one was a Samaritan!"
Ten people healed
        Only one says "Thank you!"
. . . And that one a foreigner!
Isn't it always that way?
   So little thanks for doing good?
      It's surprising that Jesus
         Didn't get discouraged!
                  . . . I sure do!
I go out of my way to do something for someone,
   And they take it for granted!
      Don't even say "Thank you!"
                  What a bummer!
    What am I, some kind of doormat?
            Everybody's servant?
Just see if I put myself out for anybody!
I don't mind helping,
    Giving,
      But I'd like to see a little appreciation!
. . . I wonder how God feels
      When I take *her* gifts for granted?
      . . . Disappointed?
            . . . Disgusted?
. . . Could *I* take a tip from that Samaritan??

Lord, forgive me for being so wrapped up
          In my own worth,
            My own giving,
   That I forget to acknowledge your gifts,
      To say, "Thank you, God,"
  For life
    For freedom
      For Jesus Christ,
        In whose name I pray.
                Amen

Proper 24 • Pentecost 22 • Ordinary Time 29

Luke 8:1-8

Hang in there!
    Be patient!
        Be persistent!
            Don't lose hope!
  . . . Good advice,
        But easier said than done!
It's so easy to get discouraged
    When things pile up,
    When nothing goes right,
    When the world seems against me,
    When prayer is not answered,
        (At least, not the way I want it to be)
    I lose heart.
I think, "What's the use?"
I see people without faith prospering,
    While I,
        Good old faithful me,
            Only seem to suffer!
I know I wasn't promised a rose garden,
    But couldn't I at least smell a flower . . .
        Once in a while?

Lord, forgive me for wanting the easy way,
        For envying those whose path seems smoother,
And give me the courage to "hang in there,"
        To follow your path
            . . . Wherever it leads,
    And to keep trusting
        As Jesus did,
            In whose name I pray.
                Amen

Proper 25 • Pentecost 23 • Ordinary Time 30

Luke 18:9-14

God, I give you thanks for who you made me!
        An American —
        A Christian —
        A responsible citizen.
    I hold a steady job.
    I live a moral life.
    I pay my taxes.
    I vote.
    I go to church . . . and give to its work.
I thank you that I'm not like other people!
        Lazy —
          Dishonest —
            Communist —
              Immoral . . .
    Or even like a citizen of the "Third World!"
. . . Listen to me!
    I *am* thankful,
        But, perhaps, I should just say,
        "God, be merciful to me, a sinner."

Lord, forgive my arrogance,
        My seeing the accidents of my birth
            As signs of special grace,
    And help me to be humble
        As well as thankful,
            To the one who gives me everything.
                Amen

Proper 26* • Pentecost 24 • Ordinary Time 31**

Luke 19:1-10

How often do I go out on a limb?
    Risk making a wrong decision?
        Looking foolish?
            Lay myself open to (possible)
                criticism?
Usually I play it safe,
    Do as little as I can get away with,
    Avoid (unnecessary) risks,
    . . . "Cover my tail feathers"
Because I know that if I'm out on a limb
        Someone can saw it off!
On the other hand,
        I'm often up a tree!
    I make one decision
        . . . usually in order to be safe . . .
    And find I've closed off my options!
        I don't have other choices!
        I'm stuck
            . . . unless someone
                something . . .
                Can rescue me!

Maybe
    Sometimes
        "Out on a limb"
            Would be better than
        "Up a tree!"

Lord, forgive me when I play it safe
    And teach me to accept risk
        For my own sake,
            And that of the Gospel.
                Amen

---

*Proper 26 may be replaced with All Saints' Sunday
**When Ordinary Time 31 falls on November 1, it is observed as All Saints' Day

Proper 27 • Pentecost 25 • Ordinary Time 32
Luke 20:27-38

Heaven!
   "Everybody talkin' 'bout Heaven ain't goin' there,"
   "Do you want to go to Heaven?"
   "Heaven came down and glory filled my soul,"
   "Heaven, I'm in Heaven,"
   "Heavenly Sunshine,"
         There are lots of songs about it,
            Lots of speculations
   All the way from golden streets
         To "pie in the sky by and by,"
         To Heaven on earth.
Heaven!
   A reward for a life well lived,
         Work well done,
   A gift
      Freely given by God
            To those who believe.
What will it be like?
   Is it worth the effort to get there?
            (If there is a "there")
     Who will go?
        Will I see my friends?
            (Do I have to take harp
              lessons?)
Heaven!
   A concept,
   A way of visualizing eternal life,
   A way of describing union with God
        (Sometimes it sounds kind of boring . . .
        If the descriptions I hear are accurate,
          I'm not so sure I want to go there!)

Lord, forgive me for "looking a gift horse in the mouth,"
     For trying so hard to define and limit your
       promise,
And teach me to accept the promise that I will live with you
And to leave the details to your wisdom.
     Give me Heaven
        Eternal life
           On your terms,
     For Jesus' sake.
         Amen

Proper 28 • Pentecost 26 • Ordinary Time 33
Luke 21:5-19

I'm afraid . . .
>Maybe not of the dark, anymore,
>>Of the "Boogeyman,"
>>Of ghosts
>>>And other childish things,

But of real things,
>Life threatening,
>Security threatening,
>>Person threatening things,

Big things
>Like war,
>Like flood,
>>Famine,
>>Earthquake,
>Like economic depressions,

Health things
>Like cancer,
>Like heart trouble,
>>. . . Like aging,

Personal things
>Like losing a job,
>>Or a home,
>>Or a mate,
>Like accident,
>>Or disease,
>>>Or crime.

I don't know who
>Or what
>>To trust!

I want to be free!
>I want to love!
>>I want to commit!
>>>I want to be thankful,
>>>>***But***
>>>>>I'm afraid.

Lord, forgive me my fears,
>My lack of trust in you,
>>In your people,

And give me courage to face life
>And grace to thank you for it.
>>In Jesus' name.
>>>Amen

Pentecost 27
(Lutheran only)

Luke 19:11-27

"Use it or lose it!"
I've heard that one before!
                                 Talents —
                                 Skills —
                                 Knowledge —
                                 Abilities —
                  Those that aren't exercised
                                 Atrophy!
That goes for gifts of God, as well!
           The parable sounds harsh
                                 But it's true!
God has given me many gifts,
      And they are intended to be used
                In God's service.
If I save them for myself
      Or refuse to use them at all,
            I am an unfaithful servant,
    And God's effort on me is wasted.
"Them that has, gets!"
                The gifts I use
                          Grow
            And I am more productive
                More useful
                          A better servant.

Lord, forgive me for wasting your talents,
            For saving instead of risking,
      And teach me to give of myself
              That I may receive joy
                      And favor in your sight.
                            In Jesus' name.
                                     Amen

Christ the King

John 12:9-19
Luke 23:35-43

Kings are easy to spot!
   (For one thing, there aren't many of them!)
     They wear velvet or ermine
         In scarlet or purple,
           Jewel-encrusted crowns of gold,
       And their bearing . . .
               Regal,
                   Set apart . . .
       They know who they are
       And show it!
But *this* king . . .
       Dressed in rags
          . . . and not many of those!
       His "crown"
          . . . a mocking ring of thorns.
"Is this any way to run a railroad?"
   It's sure not how *I'd* do it!
     (But then
        I'm not God
            . . . Am I?)

Lord, forgive my failure to understand your ways
   And teach me to see,
        Pay homage to
            Christ, my king.
                Amen

Reformation Sunday
(Last Sunday in October, Lutheran)
John 8:31-36

Reformation!
    Re-Forming!
        It's in our church heritage . . .
            We're a "reformed" church
                      (Whatever that means!)
            Is it like being a "reformed criminal"?
            Or a "reformed drunk"?
            Or maybe a "reform school"?
If I'm "formed" in the image of God,
If the church is "formed" as the "Body of Christ,"
    Why should I
        Or it
            Be "re-formed"?
I like myself
    And my church
        This way!
"Re-forming" sounds like there's something wrong
        With the old form,
        With the old structure,
        With the old person,
    Something radically wrong,
    Something that needs to be wiped out,
                Started over!
As I look in the mirror
        At myself,
        At my church,
    I know that's at least partly true.
        I'm not the person I could be,
        I'm not the person I should be,
            And my church isn't perfect either!
I try,
    The church tries,
        But we're imperfect
            In an imperfect world.
Lord, forgive my imperfection
    And my church's failings
    And recreate
        Re-form us
        To be closer to your image
            And that of your Son
                In whose name I pray. Amen

All Saints' Sunday • All Saints' Day
(First Sunday in November • November 1)

Luke 6:20-36
Matthew 5:1-12

How about that?
        A prescription for Sainthood!
        Do these things
        Be these things
    And you will be blessed,
        Beatified
    And even . . .
            In some versions
                    . . . Happy!
Some of those descriptions . . .
            Weeping,
            Mourning,
            Hungering and thirsting,
            Being persecuted . . .
        Don't sound like happiness to me!
  (But, of course,
        I'm not a saint!
        Unless you think of it,
            Not as one who is especially holy,
            But as one who tries to be
                    Faithful
    Then maybe
        . . . just maybe . . .
        I am . . .
            or could be!)

Lord, forgive me for denying my potential
        To be one of your saints,
    And give me the will
        And the strength
    To serve you faithfully,
            For Jesus' sake.
                Amen

Thanksgiving Eve / Day

Luke 17:11-19

Thanksgiving!
    Turkey and football,
        Friends and relatives,
            Parades and "groaning boards"
                (Indigestion and sugar hangovers!).
An American tradition!
    Pilgrims and Indians,
        The Mayflower and all that.
            A time of personal thanksgiving —
                For a day off from work or school,
                For the blessings of abundance,
                For too much food and drink.
    (But holidays can be a bummer!
        Too much togetherness,
        Too little activity.
            We get on each other's nerves!
Kids underfoot,
    Everybody "housebound."
                Maybe family is better
                Taken in small doses!)
Sometimes we "celebrate" because we're supposed to,
                Instead of because we want to;
And our celebration is empty and meaningless,
        Even destructive of people
            And of souls!

Lord, forgive our ungratefulness
        For life,
        For abundance,
        For love,
            For your salvation;
And teach us to be truly thankful,
        To really give thanks at Thanksgiving
    And through all of life.
We ask it in the name of Jesus,
        For whose presence we are *truly* thankful.
            Amen

Mother's Day

Mother's Day —
   A time to recognize,
      To honor,
   The source of our physical being
   And the molder of our character,
Mother.

   A word to conjure with,
   A concept that transcends culture and language —
   Nurturing,
   Sympathy,
   Support,
   Encouragement,
   Love,
      Above all
         Love.
God is a mother to us!
   Helping —
      Supporting —
         Nourishing —
            Comforting —
               Teaching —
                  Teaching kindness —
                  Teaching gentleness —
                  Teaching loyalty —
                  Teaching love —
                     Above all,
                        Love.
Mother love knows no bounds.
   It does not demand perfection
         Or beauty
         Or accomplishment.
   It is freely given
     Without reservation,
     Without question.

Lord, forgive our masculine arrogance
     (Whether we are male or female),
   And teach us to love like a mother,
     Totally
        Eternally
            As you love us.
            Amen

Annual Meeting

Annual Meeting
  B-O-O-O-R-I-N-N-N-G!!!
  Reports, elections, budgets,
  Stuff I already know
    (Or don't really care about),
  Statistics and finances
  A necessary evil (I guess),
    But not an exciting time!
I'd rather drink coffee and chat
  Or go home
    Or out to lunch
  Than deal with dull business!
But this is *my* church.
  Its business is *my* business
    (And the Lord's).
  Why can't I get excited
    (Or at least interested!)
      In what my fellow members have done,
      In what we'd like to do together
        In this part of God's kingdom?
  Is it too much the same
    Year
      After
        Year?
  Do I just want to be comforted
    Rather than challenged
      Or called to be responsible?
  Is the lack of excitement about Annual Meetings
    My lack of excitement about God's business?
Lord, forgive me my pre-occupation
  With my own affairs,
    My own wishes,
    My own comfort
  And help me to see even the mundane and mechanical parts
    of your kingdom
  With fresh eyes.
  Help me to be your servant,
    Even when I'm slogging through swamps of numbers
    And drowning in a sea of reports.
  Excite me about your church — my church
    For its sake — and my sake — and Jesus' sake.
      Amen

Installation of Church Officers

Lord, I feel inadequate.
   Your world is so big,
      So full of needs and demands,
         All clamoring for my attention,
            My decision.
   And I am so small
      One person
         Or even, in a group, less than perfectly capable,
   And yet you have called me
      To be your servant,
      To proclaim the Good News,
      To bind up the broken hearted,
      To do a particular job
         (church officer, council member, board or committee member
         — Or supporter of elected servants)
   I'm not sure I'm up to it!
I'm not a "church expert"
 (Or a financial, education or whatever expert),
   But I am charged with making decisions
      And implementing them.

Lord, give me strength!
   To speak from my heart,
   To learn my job,
   To decide and act for the good of all
      (not just for my own good),
   And keep me from becoming arrogant,
     "Power mad,"
        From forgetting that I am a servant first,
                   Leader second.
   Help me to be more worthy
      Of my position in the church
      And in all of my life;
     For Jesus' sake, who gave his life in service.
        Amen

www.ingramcontent.com/pod-product-compliance
Lightning Source LLC
Chambersburg PA
CBHW060851050426
42453CB00008B/936